THE OXFORD PIANO METHOD

PIANO TIME OPERA

arranged by

MUSIC DEPARTMENT

OXFORD
UNIVERSITY PRESS

Oxford University Press, Great Clarendon Street, Oxford OX2 6DP, England
Oxford University Press Inc., 198 Madison Avenue, New York, NY 10016, USA

Illustrations by John Taylor

Operas contain some of the most beautiful and memorable tunes ever written, and we've all probably caught ourselves humming or singing one of these famous melodies at some time or other. Well, now you can experience the thrill and fun of the opera house from your own piano stool with this selection of really easy graded arrangements of well-known arias and choruses. You could perform your favourite pieces to friends or family, but beware, they may want to sing along!

P.H.

CONTENTS

Arietta from Romeo and Juliet

Charles Gounod is best known for his *Ave Maria*, composed on top of
J. S. Bach's famous Prelude in C. This well-known waltz comes from
the opera Gounod composed in 1867.

Charles Gounod (1818–93)

Moderato

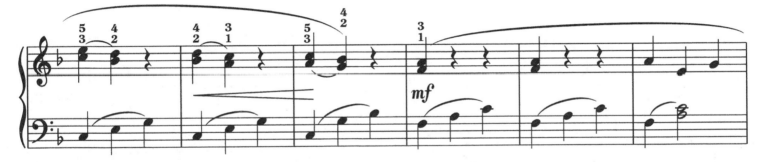

'Libiamo' from La Traviata

La Traviata has always been the most popular of Verdi's twenty-nine operas because of its many memorable tunes. At its first performance the audience erupted into laughter when the 'fragile' heroine turned out to be an enormous soprano! This piece is a jovial drinking song.

Giuseppe Verdi (1813–1901)

Allegretto

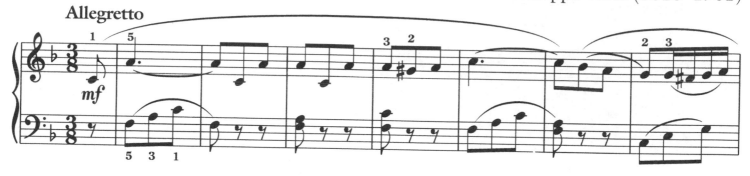

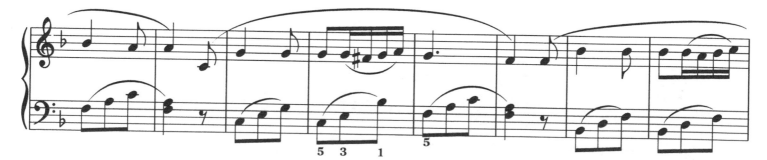

'Dove sono' from The Marriage of Figaro

The Marriage of Figaro was a failure when first performed in 1786, and closed after only nine performances. Since then it has established itself as one of Mozart's greatest works. This gracious piece is sung by the Countess, who laments that her husband, the Count, no longer loves her.

Wolfgang Amadeus Mozart (1756–91)

Andante

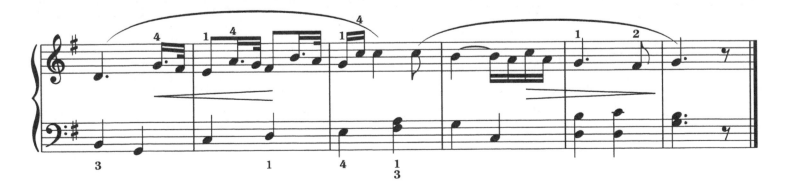

'One fine day' from Madame Butterfly

Madame Butterfly is set in Japan. It tells the tragic story of an American naval Lieutenant who falls in love with a beautiful young Japanese girl, only to leave her and return with a new American wife.

Giacomo Puccini (1858–1924)

Overture from *The Barber of Seville*

The Barber of Seville, possibly the best-loved Italian comic opera, tells the story of the rascally barber Figaro. Rossini completed an average of two operas a year for nineteen years and this opera was written in just under two weeks.

Gioacchino Rossini (1792–1868)

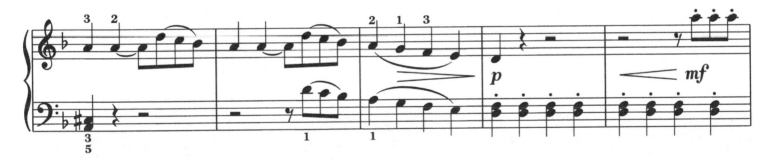

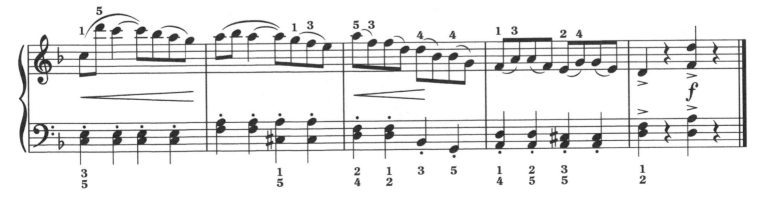

Waltz from Eugene Onegin

This famous waltz comes from the scene of a glittering ball celebrating the birthday of Tatyana, the heroine of the story, who has fallen hopelessly in love with Eugene Onegin.

Pyotr Ilyich Tchaikovsky (1840–93)

'Là ci darem la mano' from Don Giovanni

Don Giovanni has been generally accepted as Mozart's greatest opera.
This tender love song is sung as a duet between the Don and his latest
sweetheart, who unfortunately happens to be engaged to another man.

Wolfgang Amadeus Mozart (1756–91)

'O mio babbino caro' from Gianni Schicchi

Gianni Schicchi is a comic opera set in medieval Florence.
This well-known aria is sung by the heroine Lauretta, as she
pleads with her father to let her marry the man she loves.

Giacomo Puccini (1858–1924)

'The flowers that bloom in the Spring' from The Mikado

Sir Arthur Sullivan collaborated with W. S. Gilbert to produce a series of operas. Although the pair frequently quarrelled, the combination of Gilbert's witty words and Sullivan's tuneful music made their operas terrifically popular in Victorian England.

Sir Arthur Sullivan (1842–1900)

Dance from The Bartered Bride

Smetana lived and worked in Prague. He loved Czech folk music, and used some of its lilting melodies and rustic dances in his own works. *The Bartered Bride* is an opera about a peasant girl whose parents want her to marry the village simpleton.

Bedrich Smetana (1824–84)

Moderato

sempre stacc.

Gavotte from Iphigenia in Aulis

A gavotte is a stately, graceful dance in quadruple time. Gluck's opera is based on an ancient Greek drama, in which King Agamemnon decides to sacrifice his daughter Iphigenia to appease the Goddess Diana. Luckily for Iphigenia, his plans are thwarted.

Christoph Gluck (1714–87)

Chorus of wedding guests
from Lucia di Lammermoor

Lucia di Lammermoor was Donizetti's most successful opera.
It is a tragedy set in 16th-century Scotland and contains a
famous scene where the heroine goes mad. Sadly, Donizetti
himself went mad in real life and spent his last years in an asylum.

Gaetano Donizetti (1797–1848)

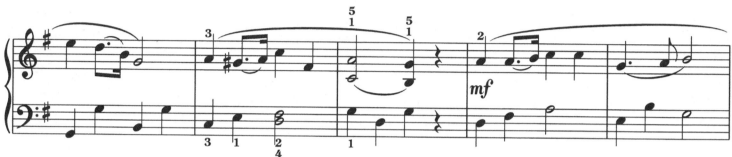

'Bei Männern' from The Magic Flute

The Magic Flute was written in the last year of Mozart's life. The fairytale plot
was very popular with the Viennese audience, with its colourful cast of a magician,
a prince and princess, priests, a bird-catcher, a serpent, the Queen of the Night,
and magic bells and flute.

Wolfgang Amadeus Mozart (1756–91)

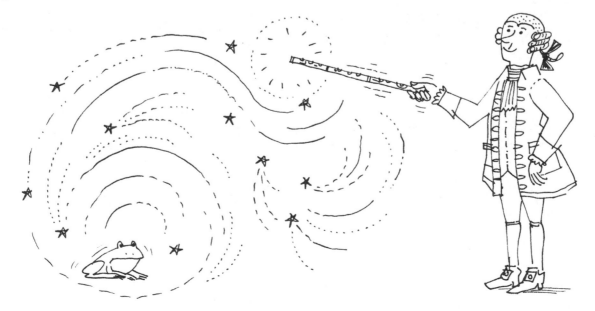

Gavotte from The Gondoliers

Here, the two gondolier brothers, who have just learned
that they are to be kings, are being instructed in the noble
art of dancing—with mixed success!

Sir Arthur Sullivan (1842–1900)

Tempo di gavotta

Pilgrims' chorus from Tannhäuser

This chorus is sung by a procession of pilgrims returning from Rome. It appears in the opera's third act, and builds to a tremendous climax, but is best known from the orchestral overture, which is often performed separately.

Richard Wagner (1813–83)

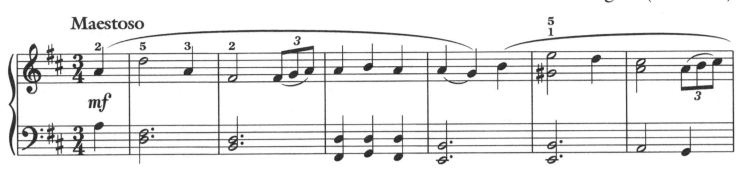

Laughing song from Die Fledermaus

Die Fledermaus ('The Bat') is a comic opera set in 19th-century Vienna.
The plot revolves around the mistaken identities and misunderstandings of the
main characters attending a fancy dress ball, one of whom is disguised as a bat!

Johann Strauss (1825–99)

March from Rinaldo

German by birth, Handel lived most of his life in England.
This was the first opera he wrote there, and a great success.
Rinaldo was leader of the crusaders, and this march was later
adopted by the Life Guards regiment as their regimental tune.

George Frideric Handel (1685–1759)

Moderato

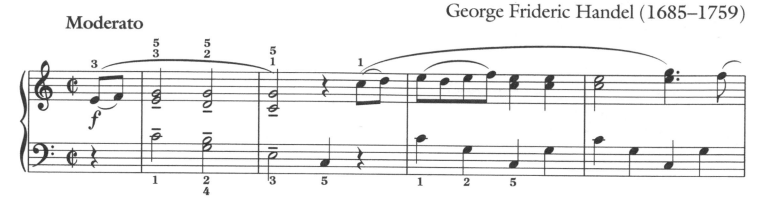

'My heart was so free' from The Beggar's Opera

The characters in *The Beggar's Opera* are a motley crew of thieves, highwaymen, and pick-pockets. The plot is set in the London underworld of the eighteenth century, and the tunes are mostly a collection of the 'pop' songs of the day.

John Christopher Pepusch (1667–1752)

Moderato

Minuet from Berenice

There have been over twenty operas composed on the story of Berenice.
Apart from this beautiful and much-loved minuet, the remainder of
Handel's opera is, sadly, rarely performed.

George Frideric Handel (1685–1759)

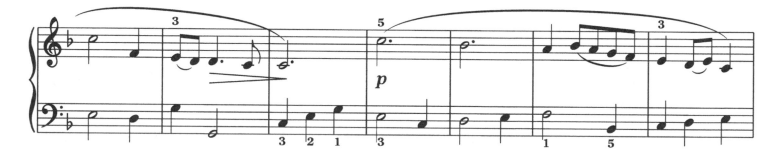

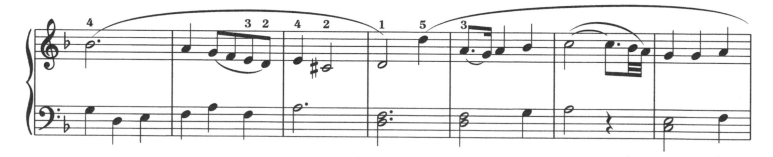

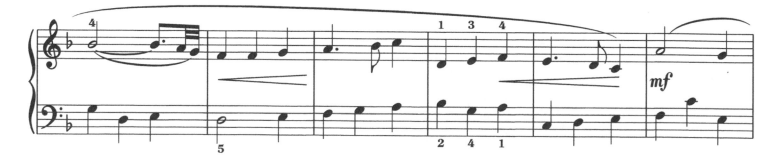

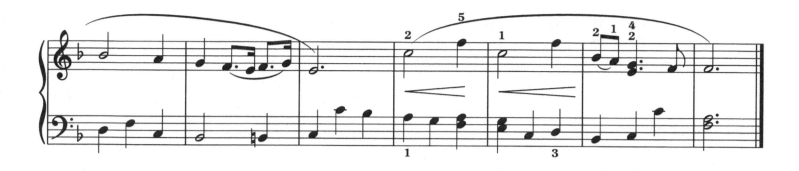

Prayer from Der Freischütz

The heroine, Agathe, prays for protection on waking from an ominous dream. Her fiancé, Max, has made a pact with an evil spirit, in return for seven magic bullets to win a shooting contest.

Carl Maria von Weber (1786–1826)

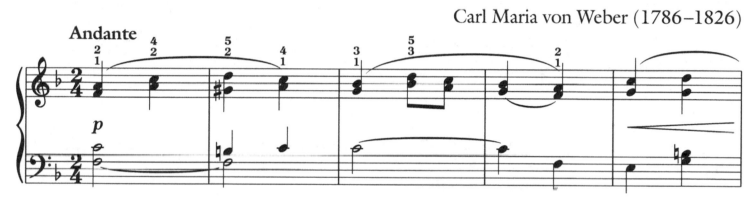

'Voi che sapete' from The Marriage of Figaro

The central character is the same Figaro who is portrayed in Rossini's
Barber of Seville. The plot is a complicated one, full of characters in
disguise, tricks, and misunderstandings. However, all ends happily.

Wolfgang Amadeus Mozart (1756–91)

Andante

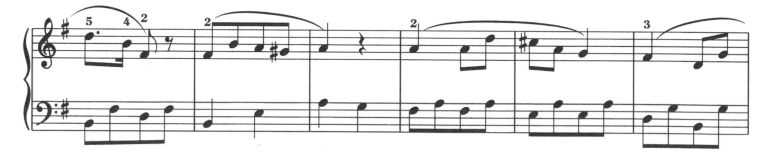

poco rit.

Barcarolle from Tales of Hoffmann

A barcarolle is a type of boating song that is supposed to have
originated from the songs of the Venetian gondoliers. The gently
rocking 6/8 rhythm imitates the motion of a gondola, or small boat.

Jacques Offenbach (1819–80)

'Where'er you walk' from Semele

Although *Semele*, like many of Handel's operas, is not often performed, this particular aria is quite well-known. It demonstrates his great gift for beautiful melodies.

George Frideric Handel (1685–1759)

Chorus of the Hebrew slaves from Nabucco

During his long life, Verdi became the most popular Italian opera composer, a member of parliament, and a national hero. This opera uses the story of Nebuchadnezzar, the Babylonian king who captured Jerusalem and took the Hebrews into captivity.

Giuseppe Verdi (1813–1901)

Bird-catcher's song from *The Magic Flute*

The bird-catcher is a character called Papageno, who charms
the birds with tunes from his pipe. In this song he merrily
sings that he'd rather catch girls than birds!

Wolfgang Amadeus Mozart (1756–91)

'Fairest Isle' from King Arthur

Henry Purcell was a choirboy in the Royal Chapel. 'Fairest Isle'
has been described as his most perfect song: play it and see!

Henry Purcell (*c.*1659–95)

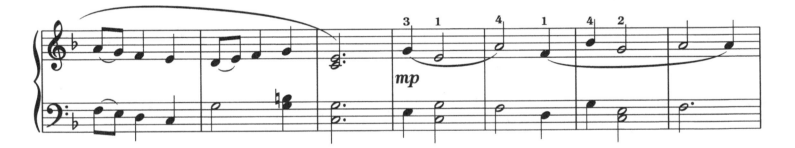

Intermezzo from Cavalleria Rusticana

An intermezzo is a short instrumental piece played between the acts of
an opera. This one comes from Mascagni's first opera, written for a
competition in which it won first prize and great acclaim throughout Italy.

Pietro Mascagni (1863–1945)

Soldiers' chorus from Faust

Gounod's *Faust* must rank as one of the world's most popular operas.
It was a particular favourite of Queen Victoria, who asked to have part
of it sung to her just before her death.

Charles Gounod (1818–93)

Habanera from Carmen

Bizet's *Carmen* is one of the world's most popular operas. It tells the story of
the gypsy girl Carmen and her rival lovers, a soldier and a toreador (bullfighter).
A habanera is a slow, sensuous dance, which was the forerunner of the tango.

Georges Bizet (1838–75)

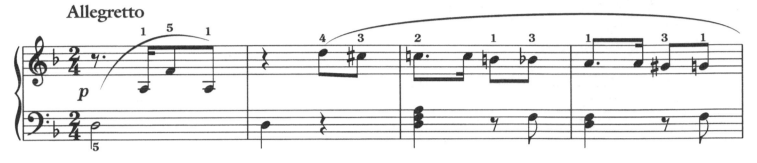

'Brother come and dance with me' from Hansel and Gretel

Humperdinck was a friend of Wagner. Only after Wagner's death did he feel confident enough in his own music to begin work on this, his most famous opera. Here, Hansel complains that he doesn't know how to dance, so Gretel teaches him.

Engelbert Humperdinck (1854–1921)

Flower duet from Lakmé

Lakmé is set in India in the mid-nineteenth century, and tells of the doomed love affair of a British officer and the daughter of a Hindu Priest. Delibes was a French composer. *Lakmé* is the only one of his operas still regularly performed, and he is now better known for his ballet music.

Léo Delibes (1836–91)

Andante cantabile

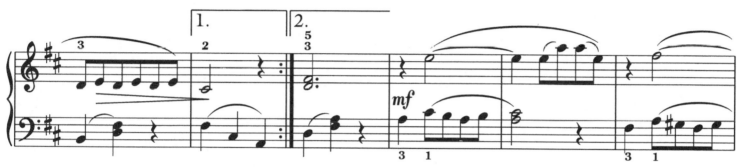

Reproduced and printed by
Halstan & Co. Ltd., Amersham, Bucks., England